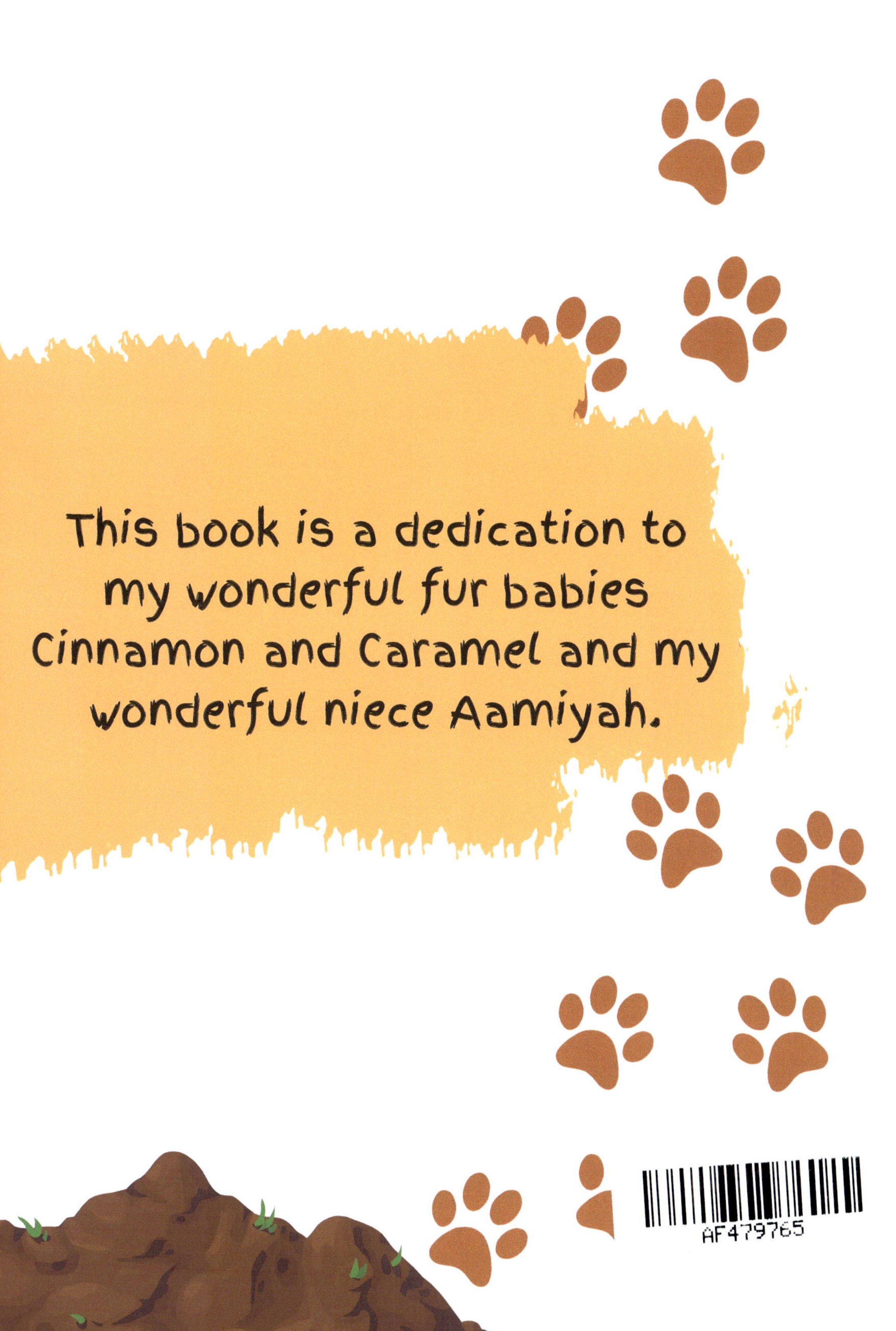

This book is a dedication to my wonderful fur babies Cinnamon and Caramel and my wonderful niece Aamiyah.

This book belongs to:

Oink! Oink! That is the sound a pig makes. Did you know pigs are very smart. A pig can learn your name in two weeks. A mommy pig can also sing to her baby just like our moms do. Best of all pigs love Tummy rubs!

Woof! Do you know what animal makes that sound? If you guessed a dog, you're right! Did you know a dog can smell forty time better that we can? Some dogs can run faster than a cheetah. And all dogs are amazing swimmers!

Cluck! Cluck! what animal makes that sound? did you know chickens can remember up to 100 faces! even more amazing they dream just like you and I. Chickens are really fast runners.

A cow says MOO! Did you know all cows are female a male is called a steer. Cows can also see almost all around them but not directly in front of them.

Bah! That's the sound our sheep makes. Did you know sheep's have rectangular pupils to help them see around them? There are over 1000 different breeds of sheep.

Purr! did you know that is a sound a rabbit makes when their happy and relaxed. Baby rabbits are called kittens. And their teeth never stop growing.

Hoot Hoot!
What's that?
It's an owl! Did
you know owls
are nocturnal?
This means
they only hunt
at night and
sleep during
the day. Owls
also can't chew!

Neigh! what was that? That was a zebra. Zebras are amazing but did you know they are considered endangered. This means there aren't many left. There stripes are one of a kind just like our fingerprints. And it helps them to camouflage and blend in to their environment.

Bellow! Bleat! That was a deer. Did you know that deer's have a really good sense of smell? A baby deer is called a fawn. Fawns also do not have a scent which makes it hard for other animals to find and hunt them.

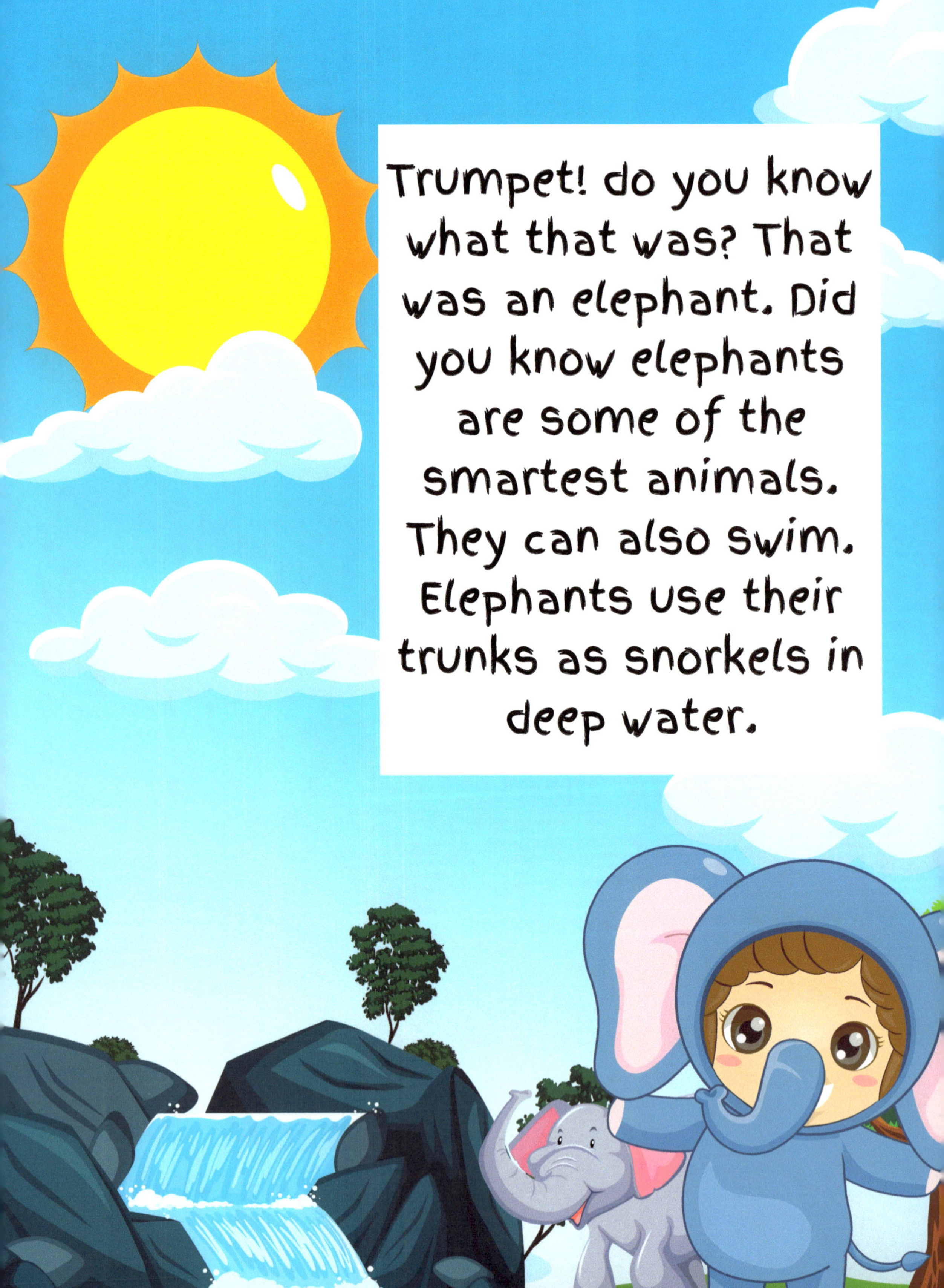

Trumpet! do you know what that was? That was an elephant. Did you know elephants are some of the smartest animals. They can also swim. Elephants use their trunks as snorkels in deep water.

Howl! What was that? That was a fox. Did you know a female fox is called a vixen. Foxes are a part of the dog family. Foxes can retract their claws.

Squeak! There goes a monkey! Did you know there are over 264 different types of monkeys. Monkeys groom each other to bond. And a mandril is the largest monkey.

Growl! did you hear that? That was a tiger. Did you know there are 6 different types of tigers.
Tigers love swimming even though they are large cats. Tigers are endangered which means there aren't many left in the world.

Roar! that was a lion!
Did you know lions
are the only cats
that roar together?
Lions are very heavy
and can weigh as
much as 30 stones.
Baby lions are called
cubs and they are
raised together.

There are so many more amazing animals all over the world that we didn't cover in this book. But, my favorite animal is the rabbit. What's your favorite?

Can You name the animals and their sounds? Lets try it together!